D1535387

THE WIFE
OF WINTER

THE WIFE
OF WINTER

* * *

Poems by Michael Dennis Browne

Charles Scribner's Sons   *   NEW YORK

821.914
B883

Copyright © 1970 Michael Dennis Browne

The following poems appeared first in *The New Yorker*: "The Delta," "Gather," "Handicapped Children Swimming," "Iowa," "Peter," "The Roof of the World," "Shopping." Copyright © 1966, 1967, 1968, 1969 The New Yorker Magazine, Inc. and Michael Dennis Browne.

Other poems have appeared in *The Bennington Review, The Iowa Review, Kayak, North American Review, Silo,* and *Tri-Quarterly.* Copyright © 1967, 1968, 1969 Michael Dennis Browne.

Acknowledgments are due to Rapp & Whiting Limited, London, who have given permission for the inclusion of twenty-five poems which were first published by Rapp & Whiting in England in a collection entitled, *The Wife of Winter.* © 1970 Michael Dennis Browne.

THIS BOOK PUBLISHED SIMULTANEOUSLY IN
THE UNITED STATES OF AMERICA AND IN CANADA—
COPYRIGHT UNDER THE BERNE CONVENTION.

ALL RIGHTS RESERVED. NO PART OF THIS BOOK
MAY BE REPRODUCED IN ANY FORM WITHOUT
THE PERMISSION OF CHARLES SCRIBNER'S SONS.

B-1.71(C)

PRINTED IN THE UNITED STATES OF AMERICA

SBN 684-10043-6

Library of Congress Catalog Card Number 74-123832

821.91
B883w

259353

*

for Eddie Browne (*1898-1960*)

"After-comers cannot guess the beauty been"

CONTENTS

PETER

Peter sleep-walks.
And is my brother.

Not knows why. But does.
Not knows why. But is.

Because my father and my mother.

And this night in pajamas
Barefoot
Left the house and walked
Five hundred yards to my sister's house
And knocked
To be let in.

Let me in. I knock.
Let me in.

And walked back,
Saying he did not remember.

I knock. Let me in.
I am asleep.

He was.

O let us in.
We are all asleep.
We are asleep, let us in.

SHOPPING

For James Tate

With the bridges of cloud cracking high
above me, I had been doing some
shopping in this odd town. I bought

Elysian hams and a pot of fruit, and
with the soft crackling of traffic in
my ears, its red sea parting for me,

I carefully tried on and finally
chose a newspaper that showed
the shape of my eyes to their best

advantage, and then I toured the dime-
store, and then out into the street
again with the green staining black

branches by the tall white
building, and the sky still silently
telling itself to collapse in big

wet bags, while from a lair
in the back of the air the first
portion of lightning licked quickly,

and I went on to buy shoes for my
Javanese cousins, an ink-stand for
Uncle Louie, and a flagellator for Auntie

Ruth who could certainly use one. The
roofs now were high tors and the
chimneys the shadows of high

pools, gripped among rock, and once
through the mist, leaning against
a parking meter, I saw, briefly, the

sun, like a desperate man, clambering
one of the roofs, sliding, frantic,
wearing the wrong shoes. And I

thought, in all this odd town there
is no way of knowing what to buy or
where in truth we are. Wine

for the cat, cakes for angels, an
elephant mask for the Catholic chaplain,
a cask of buns for the pirates I

keep concealed beneath the stairs.
And the sky above this town where
I now am, hapless, helpless, breaking

up, its white dissolution showering
light on farms, black earth, its
tipped poison streaming into weeds

that ring this town, its juice causing
strange plants to grow, and the
lakes to strain from their moorings,

to float slowly like bread's coins, to
hover over Michigan towns at night
and flash their lights, liquid

in darkness. I do not know
what to buy. In all this odd town
I do not know what to buy. Light

is crumbling on the roofs. Dark
breeds and swarms the windows.
This hot dark is amazing.

THE VISITOR

For Alex and Hanna Quaade

A fine rain falls, greening their garden.
The ladder into the apple tree drips beads of silk.
Silk rolls from the roof.

They do not play at owning.
The house is screwed well into the earth,
it holds firmly,
the foundations are good,
the earth is black and gripping.

Silk rolls from the roof.

The baby is an electric piece in their hands,
is a portion of their own exactness,
is an ease of them,
passes between them like a blueness.
Love is exact. They fit. They are three soft locks.

They have a kitchen and an orchard
and this good plot of love,
this twined intrigue of a straight marriage.

A fine Danish rain falls.

And I the guest, the friend, the foreigner,
with strange suitcase and unused energy
causing my hands to violate the slow peace
of their house.
On a darkened wet August afternoon that has simply given up.

Red books on their shelves, and purple.
The clock in the hall
springs into the pool of its sound.

A walk of ten minutes would bring me to the beech woods
which are near.

To note them is an envy.
This cannot be earned.
It comes to the hands like a cloth. It is given.

What may it be then, and what shall I take
with me tomorrow on the flight to London?
The idea of your marriage in my case?
Like a piece of wood Alex has found and painted?
Do I borrow this Danish idea?

What they have is very difficult.
Not a harbor.
Not silk. It will not swallow.

Greened is the garden, silked by the rain.
The ladder drips like a silver engine.
The apples are hard but glamorous.

I would take a scissors to my own clouds if I could,
weary of playing a Falstaff on quick visits.
I am a thin thin man.

No peace like the peace of this darkened house
in the Danish afternoon.
Christian has one tooth and sleeps.
Alex has a red book with his own Danish poems written in it.
Hanna cooks and has a hundred real skills.

A fine rain falls,
greened is their garden.

HANDICAPPED CHILDREN SWIMMING

For Lamar

A measure of freedom. Mike, floating,
would not manage so without
the red life-jacket, but would sink,

messy as weed; but with it
lies, weak, like a shirt,
and the eyes, and the tongue

uncontrolled, extended, show
the delight it is to be
horizontal on water, strapped there

by nothing but sunlight. Connie,
who otherwise moves with crutches
and stiff braces, is strong

through water. Becky, seeing always
badly, lies washed by the sense
of her own fragility, liking

the help of warm hands. Gregg
rides and plucks at the water
while Danny makes his own music

in his mind as he lilts
completely quiet. Mike's delight
opens like a flower as he floats.

He doesn't know he is floating
now in this poem. I have
nothing in fact to sustain him

and I know he will never stand
up alone. But whatever sustains
the children here is important;

inflamed with the success
of water, released, they mingle
and soften there, as wax

on wetness, limp as wet bread
on water's kindness. Those fingers
can grasp as competently at air

and water as mine. Their bodies
are milky and do not need
cleansing, except from deformity.

Water cannot wash their
awkwardness from them, water is
simple, and their defects difficult;

but they float for a while, never
as free as the times they fly
in dreams, over the cliffs

harvesting in the sea, the bats
exquisite with radar, but
something, a measure of freedom.

And Mike is lucid on water,
still physically cryptic, physically
glinting, but Mike has grace

for a while, this is his best
floating since before birth,
where he lay bunched like any

other unformed—encircled, contained,
his mother not knowing the
uncontrol of those limbs that

threshed and kicked at her
from out of that orchard of water.
Light queues to be present

as these imperfect children
float, perched rolling on
the foliage of water, shredded,

thick as May, shifting to new
flowerings of face, though their
limbs are weeds. Sunlight

9

strolls among them, padding,
healthy, firm, as our hurt
weak fleet gently disturbs the

soft clock of water. The shock
comes when you see the muscular
men who played with them

in the pool carry them
in huddles from the pool, sunlight
spreading its crime on them.

THE ORDERLY

Abel Lezcano, in Memoriam

The chair will have to wait
which was to be motorised,
because the young orderly has died.
Because the young orderly has died
the chair for Mike must wait.

Half-assembled, its other parts
holding back, but near,
it waits as if in air,
as if out in the night,
patiently, to be put together,
in the calm hum of stars.

I cannot walk into that darkened stable, his death,
I cannot remove my shoes and enter there.
But I will drive my poem, slowly, into his death,
and park it, and leave it forever there,
the motor quietly running.

CAESAR WOULD HAVE KNOWN WHAT TO DO

I hang my head, I dream, and I get back
the Danish beach, the forests trailed by mists,
the sullen out-of-season sand, and the limp Baltic.

There were no sea-walls there. There was
no place for light to lie in wait for me. There was
no light. I was an exile and at home

also on the flat North German coast, the mists
across the dunes and the early bicycles
over the thin roads between the marshes;

that early-morning water chilled their hands,
they wore capes, those gloomy water-farmers.
And their dawn home was right for me. Denmark

and North Germany, their bleak coasts, were
right for me. Caesar would have known
what to do. He would have called home his legions.

LOSING WSUI

Driving East, and I begin
to lose the string quartet put out
by University Radio WSUI;

those grave clear notes, making
a Lithuania of these black
Mid-Western fields must now

compete with blurred
upswellings of sound, tumorous
commercial heavings, as saws

sobbing into the trunks
of trees, women swaying
packed with tobacco, creaming

all the sparkling parks
their world offers. The beams
the tall transmitter spits

so strongly out near home
begin to falter now, cowards
of distance, and the rich

stream of kilowatts withers
visibly almost, a flickering
of birds turning for home

through the November air.
And now the voice of your
announcer, Larry Barrett, displaying

no panic, begins to be
sucked under by a quicksand
of muck, money music, noise

fronds at his throat, a whole
ruptured jungle of sound
springing up around the bright

tin huts our minds rent. I
will not be driven to the edge
of Iowa by the urgent

melancholy of cellos after
all. Larry is sinking
fast now, still stately, swallowed

like a pagoda. A last
gargle of vowels, and the inane
other America takes over, goodbye

WSUI, farewell Larry, remember
me to Albinoni.

THE BEAUTIFUL BOOTS OF THIRST

I see a house where no house
is, and Death

has sown there mustard-
seed, poppy, poison-plum on

the roof which is a black
meadow. The third floor

is smoke purely. I
will ascend there since

I am asked to, to the
loft of white smoke under

the dark meadow-roof, over-
long its weeds of silence.

The doors have stopped
smiling. The boots Tom is

pulling on are grinning
like craftsmen, they are

the beautiful boots of thirst.

THE DELTA

There are men making death together in the wood

We have not deserved this undergrowth
We have not merited this mud
O Jesus this mud

There are men making death together in the wood

My sergeant lies in a poisoned shadow
My friend has choked on a flower
The birds are incontinent in their terror

There are men making death together in the wood

They have taken my hands away
And they have hidden me from the moon
Pain makes decisions all around me

There are men making death together in the wood

The fish are puzzled among darkening knots of water
The ancient stairways of light sway and spill
The ferns are stained with the yellow blood of stones

There are men making death together in the wood

We have hidden the children for safety beneath the water
And the children are crying to us through the roots of the trees
They are soft pebbles without number
And they fill the streams

And the moon appears to watch now white with grief

See them now
Pilgrimming unwilling into dying
Unburdened now of blood
Their hurt bodies soaked with the dusk
See the reluctant file

In a line he leads them
In a long slow line

They leave us over the hill
They are grass
They are dust
They are shed stone
Cold as the moon

And the widow moon above
Is cold and white
And will let no lovers in tonight

THE DREAM OF THE SOLDIER

Our guns are spiked with a difficult silence

My gun hops round in a circle reloading itself

I have wound the steel of it with holly
I have stuck sprigs in the perforated barrel
I have anointed the bullets
I have kissed the stock with tinsel

I have placed my gun in an oxygen tent with intelligent
    tenderness
and I am keeping watch over it by night

This gun is my beloved father
in whom I am well pleased

All night the great bridges fell,
dripping a green rust of music.
They fell into ravines this country does not possess.
The leader has been negotiating with a foreign power
for some chasms,
to intimidate the people.

And all night the Parachutists fell, like a Pentecost.
For some, it was hours of waiting
at an intersection of air current,
denied permission to fall further,
jiggling in the night sky, not quite still, a thistle
grim with equipment.

And some fell softly but more fast, like a white
language. Falling
to meet our needs.

And they are raining on us our mothers, our dead
uncles, sisters we have had, red
Irish dogs long forgotten, orchards, farms, they know

we are in need,
and they have snowed us,
and the enemy will get nowhere near us.

The wind was wet
    with the easiest wounds
I tore up the paths
    for difficult bandages

I revolved on a bush
    like a turkey unclothing
I pumped a pullet
    with bullets of milk

I counted the guilty
    I killed in my sleep
Their blood streamed over
    the fences like sheep

The soldier comes to me
He is a tenor

He is a shining bullet
in a casing,
a husk of green cloth

Carve my hands
      they are bread
Pack my legs in a flask
      they are coffee
Wrap me up   Pour me out
Feed the earth, I wish it
wet with my meaning

Choose me a neighborhood of bullets

Set fire to the dog pound
      for my family

Photograph birth
       from a great height
Take stills
       of my breathing
Apply hotels to my temples
       in torture

Unless you put your hands in my wounds
and most surely the wounds of these men,
unless you should so do
we will not believe you

Wash me in orders
       Read me hot chocolate
Tape up my germs
       Grow me again in a greenhouse
Mount me
       Cut me down

The rains suffer heavy casualties
the rains are raw and new
the rains stiffen

Blow my nose with a battalion
       Chew my gun till it sounds good
Feed me Yugoslavia
       Beget me Hawaii
Christen my children Illinois
       Hang Copenhagen from these branches

Have the whole platoon
washing its weapons in death

My wounds excreting silver

The bombs breathing on the water three times
The bombs bleeding on the water

Each bomb is a hermit tortured through and past pain

The bombs exchange shirts on the way down

Now this   and this   easy it is easy   snow as

Call to us   come to us crying
we
will not rise again

Orbit a satellite under the earth:
do the dead repose, O tell me,
in radioactive belts,
and will we ever be suited
to travel there, through and beyond
the rings and coils of our dear dead
to the hot moon earth's core?
O you will need special clothing
not to be contaminated
on the lengthy excursion through your dead.

I have mailed letters to all my wounds
informing them they are disgusting
I have arranged citations for wild geese
who chose to fly south
I am having my wife enlarged

I have issued weapons to pianos
I have set the cinemas adrift
to float burning and sow panic among
the slow fleets of civilian opinion
I have arranged alarming armadas of sunlight

The reservoirs have gone berserk
          and are spilling the beans to the enemy
the city parks have thrown up their green and gold
                    golf courses in horror
the motels are out on their own roofs
watching the night sky for signs

The White House has been holed below the water line
          and is sinking fast

the archives are shifting dangerously
the hands of thirteen million secretaries
                        are being held as hostages
the skirts of the women of America
                        have been raised to the patriotic maximum
as they wade the sexual waters of war

I am out of the hearing of bleeding

Looking down on the fighting from a great height
I find my mouth filled with moss
which is burning

My tongue has been sent for
my hands are standing by

Clothe my body in the information
                        you have brought back
Read between the lines of the enemy

Take my hands away carefully
I have no others
Blow my feet off beautifully
The only I own

I have an ear for language
Remove it gently

Your fingers touching the map
bruise it.
The globe of the world
is eye so veined with countries
it cannot see.
Asia is a cataract.
The Pacific is a rigid tear.
Africa is a scar for ever.
I may not tell you of the shape
of the Americas.

Asia has cut off its ear
and sent it to us.

I stamped on the burning wheat
and the wheat was a child;
the water was living in rings
and the eyes of the water were wild.

Toward evening we sat in the willows and village
                    drinking our guns
I hanged a gnat from the roof
                    of a hut with my belt

This is a child
This is a pig
This is foam

Obey it

A great wind
crawls through the wounds of these children
green limbs of them
green hair of them

I hear the groves of wounds at the water's edge

Unless you put your hands in such wounds
and most surely the wounds of these children
unless you should so do
we will not believe you

No wound has a still center

Each wound has a liquid eye, watching
Each wound has doors that will not heal

The trees see fit to wither

I have seen the planes come,
and the tall hands of their commanders.

But most of all did I see, as their long loads fell,
Age, in search of his lost sons, climbing there,
mounting with fevered eyes through those falling stairs,
seeking, in the dark that is newly come to light,
Hope, Belief, Expectation and Love,
his maimed irretrievable children.

THE ROOF OF THE WORLD

He is making love with his wife on the roof,
that's all right.
But sixteen years . . .
The cattle wait around as long as they can,
then go off, like grenades.
The neighbors get heated over breakfast,
but they won't come down,
there's no legal loophole.
If a man wants to spend as much time as that
on the roof of his house with his wife,
that's all right by the law,
there's nothing improper in that.
Sometimes they noticed the grass beneath them,
and the woods around that, change
in their colors, the summer's
thin strokes, the slow
flood of fall blood, and the townspeople
that lay down and died like ticks,
but they didn't care.
That was sixteen years well spent,
he said, she said, as both
at last came down,
to the gold of garbage,
to the piano an oak again,
the television a camera,
the dog a frog,
and the huge children they had forgotten about
waiting around minutely, in baskets,
to be born again.

IOWA

Air as the fuel of owls. Snow
unravels, its strings slacken. Creamed

to a pulp are those soft gongs
clouds were. The children

with minds moist as willow pile
clouds purely in their minds; thrones

throng on a bright mud strangely
shining. And here

chase a hog home as a summer sun
rambles over the pond, and here run

under a sky ancient as America with
its journeying clouds. All their hands

are ferns and absences. Their farm homes
on their hills are strangely childlike.

IOWA, JUNE

From my front wheels the scared rabbits
sprouting. The ditches

piled with bleached squirrels. The sky's
slow tumescence, the dark
delivering its flowers.

Who now a house has
must lie there in silence.
Who now a wife has
must guard her unbreathing beside him
in the house,
                     the tower of the house,
as the nettles pass the window,
dryly tapping, and the stunned

moths plummet past the drifting
fireflies, trailing their
                     canyons of gas, into
the dark grass. In the far
pasture a foal noses the oak's

growing shadow.
                     Fathers
are losing their sons this night. Your wife,
O keep her, in the dead sea
of your own sweating as your dream

blazing and loaded lifts off
from the light-wet runway, to where
no tower of her touch may recall you,
where your sons are finally
grasslands waving unduly
                     beneath you. She is there

for you still, in the drift of branch
in the dark, enter her as the sea
from the shore of yourself, hold
to her still through the vast
anchors of sand, rising.

In the house, the tower of the house.

BICYCLE

Edward, rainwater, and clouds
Edward, rainwater, and clouds

I wish the love affair could be
reduced to a bicycle;
now, I could ride that.

The dream did the best it could.
A bishop blessing his own lungs,
a bird who saw
a target through the window and flew for it.
The bird was in the room first.

I could come in
because he was in Eugene.
'He is in Eugene.'
But still you were cooking
for George the landlord.
'I must cook for George yet.'
the
clothes, dance movements.

All roads
to you, all farms I
ride past still
within a room.

The children came out of
an alley of my childhood,
an internal
Dickens avenue.

Edward, rainwater, and clouds
Edward, rainwater, and clouds

Elizabeth Surly & Edward Comprehension,
their first appearance.

WINDOWS

The sun comes through the red windows
and through the blue it comes. Breakfast
is out of the question. Fists
shudder and close like hoses. Four
jolly monks blow their minds on cider. An ant
crawls out of an egg, very angry.
Let there be answers.

When Love has done, and is finished finally,
the tongue puts down roots
in a new mouth. Cars

are driven out to the hills
over the town, snow comes down
in the shape of a shrine. You
do not need to go to the Arctic
for the refrain of a new song; it is

a squire's great house
collapsing among its rich estate;
elms can be seen to shiver,
and the kings in the fireplace
burn up with small gold cries. What

we have all done inside the new building
is to teach Love,
of Love's ways, what is. I am descending
with my students now,
with every possible window in my pocket.
In the last resort I am naked,
the town is fit for this:

my friends over the water cannot hear me,
and who am I
not to hear them, when my heart
is filled with ears, of all kinds?

I wish I could love you immediately,
but the sun is too strong
through the green windows, and I am
lit up and utterly fine.

LA FILLE AUX CHEVEUX DE

Connecticut darker

I want to be totally your cousin
I want to sleep on my left side
I want to sleep in the smallest bed in the house
in the furthest highest room under the roof
I want to fit into a niche like a saint who's a statue

Do not touch me I am my own garden

The trees have dappled masses haven't they
Small winds rise from our own roses
The trees hiss as they lift the wind does that
The trees with windy hiss

I am only a ferry
I go backwards and forwards only
not your journey
not your journey

I will cook your breakfast and I will wave to you by daylight
But by night I will be moss I will be a cabin and private
I will suck on the thumb of my fear

The trees mingle with the air and sunlight they are a mixture
The butterflies rock their small thrones along the paths
I've the spine of a bride
Plants we are small are we ivy and fern
Roses don't concentrate

If you want to come on any excursion
Such as to the quarry
Such as to the shopping center
Such as for stamps

I saw the squirrel he is a bridegroom grappler popular with
                                     the branch
I saw myself in the grass I was small I was a half
I saw myself in the fire I was of gold and ancient

Pray for me for the hair I pray my range
You can't come up to me here
Dear cousin your portrait your bones your old trees

AS IF THE EARTH I WALKED ON

For Bill and Ada Beth Lee

As if the earth I walked on.
As if this grass,
these trees over the water,
this tree which is called white alder.
As if this warm evening, with the ash in its air.

As if this earth I walked on,
its shapes and forms.
Strangers in the garden, bended among.
Or tread the grass with unaccustomed quiet,
knowing myself a stranger
and a dying one here.

As if all who wish might be here.
Let them come, admit them,
let them come up out of the earth.
The arm is a branch in such darkness.
As if the earth I walked on.
As if I was not ever here,
nor grass, air, nor the white alder tree.
On us all the slow ash falls.

I wear the great robe Need.
And Heart, you float in a strange dark land,
loneliest of riders.
As if the arms of my mind turned
to my own body, from a great distance,
as if my arms did not rise in such ash!
As if I knew. As if the white tree were
my other self, a father from darkness,
or Dark Brother, dead one.
As if the mind did not shine!

And the earth I have walked on,
this evening, and by the water
the white alder tree, the gloom in the grass,
and the soft fine fall on us all
through the night of the slow snow ash.

Los Angeles

Voices out of the night;
I mean the telephone operator
in Putney, the short wave,
the girl on the record.
Voices out of the night, *who are they.*
Where did the voices go.
An iron lies in a glade
giving off blame.
The body hangs together as it can,
the water boiling behind it.
Floats. What do you mail in the box,
what do you matter.

TWO BIRTHS

FOR CAITLIN LALLY
(BORN FEBRUARY 1968)

I heard a bird
    From a gold tree sing:
"This is the beginning
    Of everything."

And then a worm
    From the dark earth spoke:
"This is the morning
    That I awoke."

And so I walked out
    In the world of man:
With the worm, I awoke,
    Like the bird, I began.

FOR TIMOTHY CARSE GAINES, ARRIVING THREE WEEKS
LATE, FEBRUARY 1969

Nine months in branchy darkness stored
Can make a fellow fearfully bored;
And so at last, deciding to be,
Timothy Carse came down from his tree.

ONE CHRISTMAS

It would snow, Angela thought.
It snowed round our house.
I *ran* through that dark,
I pressed the door-bells
of a dozen neighbors and ran,
their dogs after me. This was
Elgin Road, Weybridge. From here I see

that small boy wicked
in the night and snow, I see
my father the bush of black
shiny holly, I see his death
planted by gardens, and snow
that dropping cannot dry
the grief of that house, nor its red
brick, nor the blood of it. I think

to run after him, that boy, down
those familiar avenues. I
go then, I begin to pant
down the lengths of that
speechless dark. But I do not
catch him ever.

THE WIFE OF WINTER'S TALE

She lies by the man her husband
in the high white bed,
their breathing through the dry dark farm,
his head near her head.

But far from the farm in the hills,
under the moon's strange stare,
the wolves in hardest December
cry out through the frozen air.

The farm sleeps dark on its slope,
the woman lies by the man,
but she is not with him there,
not under his breath or his hand

but out in the far clear cold
hills where he may not go,
where she and her glistening lover race
over a murderous snow.

THE WIFE OF WINTER

*The thoughts of a farm wife from
dawn to midnight of a winter day*

For music by David Lord

1. WAKING

Dark. A new dark. I am dropped
from the high claw of a dream. Fox

retrieves me, wolf waits.
Who is the owl with wings of snow?
And where is my eagle now?
He is not here, my lady they cry.
In the hills, O my lady they cry.

How strange the sky is.

One horse stands, a ghost
with an eyelash of diamond.
The sky hangs like a gray garden.
My bones are so deep in my hands,
who would ever hear them?
How my arms rise.
O farm in a white sea!
We have a whole foam-load of snow!

I who was fine once,
with eyes of October,
with skin of snow,
where should I look for love now,
where should the wife of winter go?

2. MORNING

I am the woman of white shell
Once again I am perfect

It is eagle at my window
It is wind at my door

The house is becoming simpler
Now it has thought of me

See my house now feed from my hand
How my ribs of grain glisten

In October he came,
on a calm clear day;
I was the wheat white with waiting,
a field for the wind to walk through.
White farm, white farm,
tall your shadows grow;
far field, far field,
your fixed furrows flow.
Birds through the air.

Each cloud is a pure branch,
each wood is wet with sunlight,
the cattle glitter in dappled camps,
the crow flaps stiffly from the hill,
the fox a fond eater.

O house
Am I the enemy you ordered?

I declare fox on my mother who is distant
Wind at my door which is listening

My hands a small
and perfect snow

What wrecked ships drift in this head
What dead seas swallowing their farms

3. BIRD

A bird has come, a red
barrel-breasted puffed one
with a quick claw.
He is nimble about bread,
he is good at light loads.
O he can carry a crumb over acres,
his wings never stumbling,
he picks his way
through the flake-falling,
he lifts up into the gray
eye of winter air
with his victory of crumb.
He will not come down to me easily.
It is his hunger only
that brings him down.

And another bird calls in the night
"No love, No love, No love"
over fields of snow.

And eagle comes to me,
as the children sleep,
as *he* sleeps,
and we climb together over these fields:
the owl senses us only,
the fox has a notion
in his swift picked way through the wood.

"No love, No love, No love."

4. MAN

A man has stepped out of a tree,
all will be lost with me.
A man has come
with arms of oak,
with his hands of ash.
A man has stepped out of a tree,
all will be lost with me.

In a calm he comes,
in a dark.
Gold of his head,
his steps steady.
A man through the wood walking.
In a calm he comes,
in a dark.

What are the steps
of this man through my mind?

O sleek my darling, my oak of silk!
O steep my love, my elm of pouring!

A man has stepped out of a tree,
all will be lost with me.

5. AFTERNOON

May I come now?
And may I come soon?

My room is lit with an ill light.
Shall this house be so?
Shall I, so?

My heart has filled with its own
deep evening air.
I hear the foot on the stair,
the float of the dark,
the sound of the dew at my heart.

I have gone out over these fields
a hundred times,
vague with the illness of this snow.
I do not know
from what sky this farm
like some calm fruit fell.
And how many years I have gone
through these rooms,
and how many winter days and afternoons,
and how arranging,
and how preparing.

The sky has no fault now. Hiss
of the sun high
over snow,   its gas of yellow. The woods,
their birds,   soft as chalk their wings,   timber
in their glow,   tumble,   the dark
starting, the snow
beginning again
like a sighing without sound.

As snow falls, I fall;
as light fails over the fields, I fail;
the tides of dark drift in,
my heart floats through me
like an evening,
trailing no anchors.

6. THE CHILDREN

The children run to me over the snow.
Their hands, with the odor of apples!
Their eyes, with the smell of stars!

The birds follow, feeding on welcome.

O my children,
the snow will fall
over the edge of the world,
I will be with you.

Tell me,
is our farm's taste sweet to the finger?
Is the turned earth inky and glistening?
May I be your mother?

7. NIGHT

The bell of dark
hangs in the tower
unbroken

and I ask of the man
who is by me   who
are you   stranger   who are you

who entered me   why do you lie
in me unbroken   in a sleep
of blood   all the food

of the dark in you   why
this strange harvest   this clear
disease of water   why fear you

How should I touch you,
how should I know
what dawn the dark of your eyes will want?
How should I come to you,
how should I find
that small house of your heart
among such hills?

The moon sleeps in the boat of a branch,
and *he* sleeps, his hand in my hair,
but I do not know him.
Under me I hear
the hills drop away,
and their snows staggering up into the night,
where no birds will be,
no owl for me, no eagle;
but I pray the cold claw
of the dream come down, as I lie,
my white world around me;

and let me be borne,
over these fields,
from this dark house to my bed
in the frost-bright brambles of cloud.

I hear his claw through the air.

AND THIS FOR YOU

and this for you my wandering one
wherever you are whether it is
the white farm or on the crown

of the road in the red car or
hiding sun's needles in haystacks
before evening prods wayside

hedges to stone and this for
you whenever as well, if five
years or more looking back or

down across at me or up because
for you my wandering one all roads
you take are gripped in my mind's

hand, I possess all maps you ever
will need, countries cross, I know
all rivers' shallow spots, come

to me for counsel, you are going
to have to come my wandering
one some day, come sooner then

GATHER

Sometimes still wet from the shower
she will come to me to lie by me,
saying she could not wait to be with me,

and then do I take her head in my hands,
gather all to her grace, the fields
of my childhood, all songs I have sung,

all hill-paths taken, all evenings
among friends, the summer waters, the flame
of the white farm, the filling of all flowers,

her head in my hands, her eyes wide, gather
all that I was and am, all I shall be,
and love.

THE TERRIBLE CHRISTMAS

All day the snow.
Fell. All day the snow fell,
navy-blue and fatal to goats.
                    In each

farm drifting helplessly the
graying wives grip vast

rudders of bacon, desperately.
Mailmen die

giggling in deep drifts,
geese in the furthest south
can be heard braying as they
                    unseasonally mate. On

the first night I climb
to the roof with my wife, a
ladle clenched between my
teeth
        as dark

rolls in with its soft mucky
waves from the north. We lie

on the roof breathing as
bluely the snow strokes us
        The chimneys look good. Far
off, over other hills, we know

our neighbors are having
a bad time of it. Then, out of

the snow, little
lamps beginning to wink, snails
floating. So many

parcels from Africa, such
ivy to harvest. I

kiss her all through
Christmas on the roof,
                    the snow

sighing around us like pirates
with soft trousers . . .

THE LAST DAY BUT ONE OF THE WORLD
or
GOING TO BE THERE

One cloud hangs a perfect udder;
the nettles stand very straight in the sun,
the hot hay jangling
like brass in the barns.

The birds are turf-sweet and swift,
the lashes of blades lower.

The jar shall be my judge.

I hear the sunlight at work
on the water. The water
is heightened under my eye,
I have arranged everything with this

water in mind. Who
will drive my father in herds
through the milk-dark underworld, who
will beat the moths from my mother? In the

blent wool of the lamps the
moths are thick as motes; when will
the light not clog them then?
                                        Thunder

hangs in the bud, the robbers
are not yet born, they are

moths of the womb who snow
when they should not, who flicker
the rinks of black ice.
                                        Bees
beat plums' drums, the yellow nettle

lies down with the tulip, sunlight
suits the orange foxglove,
the rains are going round
in smoke and air is a third

of the world as she
takes off her body (air
is the whole of evening, the
water of woodsmoke) as she
draws the moon from off her and it
rises, yellow, extraordinary, out of

the plum black blood

wet water. This is the last moth-
thick day but one of
the world as she
unpins an Empire, it falls in folds, this

is the reallest place on Earth, I am going
to be there.

SLEEPING ON THE MOON

The bulb hangs in the hot dark
like a white blood-drop.

All night, all night I meet you
at the airport, all night I am

cycling down the shaking tunnel
of trees, threshing with shadows,

my arms are paper, my eyes
shells the dark coils in, like sea.

It is odd at the airport, crammed
as limbo. The wound on my head

hurts me, how it throbs. And I
wake to find I have been sleeping

on the moon, on a bare bench.
I am covered with old newspapers!

A SONG FOR THE LAST WEEK-END

*(Following a Fierce Discussion
of Form & Content)*

I plucked a berry, I plucked a flower,
I planted an owl in an oak in an hour;
I found a lake at the end of its tether,
I swam out of hand in a field full of weather.

And all for the lady and dancing,
And all for the silk-fine bush of her head,
And all for the birds
And the far better words
That for skill's lack, not love's,
I never have said.

I opened my heart and I emptied my mind
Of each fresh-grown fever, first feeling and find;
May this set her prancing,
May this keep her warm,
And may the sweet fair be content with my form.

THREE SONGS

I

In Paris, in August, when I was young,
I wooed a woman with silver tongue;
The song was the sweetest ever I sung,
In Paris, in August, when I was young.

Her name is love, love is her name,
Never again can I be the same;
Poor I the moth, fair she the flame;
Her name is love, love is her name.

II

I slept in sheets of sanity
But my blankets all were mad;

The windows dreamed they had parted
And woke to discover they had;

The wind flew in like a kitchen
And tied up the clock in a knot;

I dreamed my true love had entered,
I wakened, but yes, she had not.

III

Playing tennis in the snow
With my true love, most gladly I

Did let her win each game, each set;
I praised her grave, inaccurate eye,

And proudly as she leapt the net
Did raise her in that world of snow

And sing the song all lovers know.
Six Love, Six Love, do such games go.

SONGS FOR CHILDREN

There was a ship set out to sea,
    Dark the waters and deep,
And it was made from a tall oak tree,
    Silver the clouds and steep and O
    Dark the waters and deep.

The ropes were soft as sparrows' bones,
    Dark the waters and deep,
The sailors as hard as cherry stones,
    Silver the clouds and steep and O
    Dark the waters and deep.

The flags like flowers were pink and white,
    Dark the waters and deep,
The captain's eyes were as black as night,
    Silver the clouds and steep and O
    Dark the waters and deep.

The ship set out on a northerly tack,
    Dark the waters and deep,
It sailed from sight and it never came back,
    Silver the clouds and steep and O
    Dark the waters and deep.

   *

O I can sell you a talking plum
I can sell you a squeaking rose
I can hire you a horse as thin as your thumb
    But you'll have to pay through the nose the nose
    O you'll have to pay through the nose

O I can give you a grinning fish
I can give you an apple that snows
I can find you a king who is fit for a dish
    But you'll have to pay through the nose the nose
    O you'll have to pay through the nose

O floating foxes O squirrels that sneeze
O world that nobody knows
O I can give you whatever you please
    But you'll have to pay through the nose the nose
    O you'll have to pay through the nose

※

My uncle lives in an acorn,
He likes to live that way;
When I hear a breeze in the tops of the trees
I see my uncle sway.

Up my uncle into the clouds
And down my uncle again;
When he smells the snow on the branches below
He rolls his eyes in the rain.

※

I sleep on a pillow of water
My cousins are silver fish
I love the mayor's daughter
I eat from a wooden dish

I run in the meadows for pleasure
I sing to the birds in the trees
I eat and I sleep at my leisure
I never cough nor sneeze

The mayor's daughter is soft as sky
I shall marry her on a cloud
The fish will leap the cattle fly
And the flowers sing out loud

※

O who now sees the blind black bat
Wipe the moonlight from his wing?
O who now sees the midnight stream
Whose pebbles underwater sing?

O who now sees the clumsy bee
Breaking open the yellow rose?
Who tastes the cherries from the moon?
Who hears the doors of water close?

Who sees the spiders dance in secret?
Who sees the meadow-flowers turn blue?
Who can sing the night-owls' language?
Who sees? Who hears? Who knows? O who?

A lady walking in an orchard
Met a goat tied to a tree.
"O goat" the lady cried astonished,
"Why are you tied, pray tell to me."
           White the blossoms, the blossoms white.

"Alas I once was young and handsome
But a wizard put a curse on me;
There is nothing that can restore me
But a kiss from a fair lady."
           White the blossoms, the blossoms white.

Instantly she bent and kissed him
And there uprose a shining fog;
Beside the lady a goat no longer
But a young and handsome smiling frog.
           O white the blossoms, the blossoms so white.

The clouds with silenced engines drift
The trees seethe with their birds
The river is thick with its currents
And my heart is thick with its words

My body is glad with dancing
My mind is filled with trees
The shadows are scattered through meadows
My heart is down on its knees

The river sweats under moonlight
The deer steps down through the wood
The air is energy always
The white thorns warn me of good

The warm stones float up in welcome
The water is strong to the touch
The water thrives in its ripeness
I love all rivers too much

Air in all angles delights me
The antlers of currents creak
The fish are rising to chorus
The air has not slept for a week

I have wiped my face with sunlight
And turned my back on my face
The sun is a mansion of madness
The moon is a restless place

I have broken the sunlight in pieces
I have crumbled the moonlight like grass
I have sold all my candles to camels
I have watched the weasels pass

The wind will pitch jewels in passing
The flowers will scatter their praise
Energy answers my meaning
I'll dance to the end of my days

A SONG FOR CHILDREN POSSIBLY

O never shake hands with snow
Unless it invites you first;
Once I made a mistake
With a horrible flake
And it wasn't the flake came off worst.

O never take tea with an apple
Unless you are sure it is wise;
He may be a bore
Or bruised to the core
Or a serpent in subtle disguise.

O never go swimming in April,
For April is terribly deep;
Be sure that you know
How to bellow and blow
Or to bleat like a bee in his sleep.

O never dance tangos with rhinos,
Although they may seem very sweet;
They simply can't sing
Or do anything,
And those bastards will *ruin* your feet.

THREE

THE MICHAEL MORLEY POEMS

For Roy & Margaret Watkins

"Michael Morley, he's no good,
Chop him up for firewood."

"Hush, hush, whisper who dares,
Christopher Morley is saying his prayers."

MICHAEL MORLEY

Did not stay in his room dark alone all Christmas
But wanted to
(he though, for a while, being silly)
Don't be wrong in your head, come out
of your barn
Silver barn a'm going now but w'ill be back
This 'poem' is called
The Silver Barn

MORLEY'S CHRISTMAS PRESENTS

One pair gloves.
Two white scarves.
One record of Richard Wilbur (Richard Wilbur?)
reading his own poems.
And learning that the moon is really very
very gray.

THE WHITE GODDESS

Morley, learning that the moon
was gray, poured himself
a drink.
A big drink.

CHRISTMAS 1968

The skull of Christmas is bright white!
Mr Morley the toy
sits in a chair, looking a little like
William Blake, but lacking his skills.
The snow has wrapped
its presents badly.
And wind roars through
the Verrazano Narrows Bridge.
And even God is, secretly, a little fed-up.

APOCALYPSE

"O for the witch to be sexy!"
thought Morley,
snowbound in Connecticut.
The hills of Vermont
open their doors; out step
cows proudly sporting cuff-links;
she's done it again!

A man in a white jacket
conducted the wind in the woods.
The man of glass asleep in the car
was touched & he cracked

Seeds drifted out of the glass man
& settled on the snow

Pipes of the hand froze
Blow into the glass hand!
Blow into the glass hand!

The neighborhood of white houses
is stored & silent on its sites

In a closet a man muddled
his own grocery

The wind fitted a man into a mail-box

Morley firm & fantastic!
A great dog lies out in the snow.
Dead, full of presents.
He is Morley maybe.

INVALID

Are you an invalid, Morley?
Are you sick, boy?

The fire dances in the grate
like a merry man.
He's a Viking,
he hopped from a sleek moving ship.

If the motorcycles came to you
& kissed your sleeves,
would you get up?

No, I wouldn't.

MORNING

mocks me,
who am Michael Morley, broiler
of fine bacons.
He who burned the barn.
He who fell from love with a thump.
I hear his windows melted.
Why doesn't he go to Denmark?

The organist has lost his pencil-sharpener,
the mechanic is trapped in the pipe.
What are those tracks in the snow round the house?
Birds? *The devil's reading list.*

Morley flushes the frozen john with wine.
Morley's gloves lie out in the snow,
like claws somewhere.
He does not understand
the heating system of his house or mind.
Why the pipes froze, will freeze again.
Poor heart.
He runs in circles like an aerodrome.

'Come out to a party' the phone sings.
Oh no, thinks. I think
I will just stay here & shit gently.

A man wipes Morley's windows, thinking
he is going a long way. I am not
(thanks, man) going that far, thinks Morley.
I am not going that far.

THE LAST DAYS OF MORLEY/RILKE

"He sleeps in the heated house of friends"

He sleeps with three mouths.
One arm is flung up against the wall.
Beyond the wall
the sea, a range of Alps. A candle of animals.
He sleeps in the heated house of friends.

The womb on the table.
The madman's smile sweet.
The mailman soaks.
An animal comes to him with a lighted candle.

Who sleeps with the sea near his hands?
One fingernail Provence,
one knuckle a winter there.
If the palm of a hand is a window
the landscape seen through it is the Principality of Wounds.

What lights lie down in the snow to die,
flashing?

So, Manager, the dark farm, Death,
chalk-like, wearing
the apron of slow vipers. White
porridge. Light buttermilk.

You lie, the satin guitar now,
the incompetent bracelets of worms.
A view of a formal garden with stained statues & hills beyond.

An Alpine mailbox containing flowers & the head of a young
    girl.
A valley, where your noisy death clatters like the river.
An Alp, where your death is the snow dropping.

The self of friends. Heat.

THE CHRISTOPHER MORLEY STADIUM

At night
& in moonlight
Michael Morley runs
in the Christopher stadium
with no one around.

On such a night as this
did Morley run.

Puff, puff, am I my brother's keeper,
Puff, puff, this age has no miracles.

Pant, pant, the white spikes
puff in the moonlight.
Ambience of far things.
I am a flea in the hair of the dark god.

And so all night
in the dark gold Christopher stadium
Michael Morley runs.

THE SEA

The sea.
I went down to the sea.
I went down into the sea

because my city is there.
But I foundered on the beach.
I walked around in the white house
of my reason. Nerves at the wrist
opened. And truth
fondled me
like never before, until I was
hard, like the nettle of all failures.
And women burned on my hands and feet,
and sea birds shattered on the street.

MORLEY & MOHAWK AIRLINES

I saw the earth below me,
its farms & cloverleafs.
    A drunk stewardess clawed her way past me.

Looking down I saw
the terrible border between Connecticut & Massachusetts,
its policemen itching with fire, their radios writhing.
    One engine blew its nose, it had a canned handkerchief.

I saw a storm deciding on a farm
& a town laid out like a bloody letter E:
I saw foam on the chin of a mayor
trapped in a field by its enraged barley.
    A steak went by in a meal, breathing heavily.

I looked down & I saw enough ammunition
to put the ear of God to sleep
& children pretending to be streets
misdirecting their friends down mine-shafts & well-holes.
    And I pulled the plug out of the airplane.
    And the airplane turned into a fish, & went on swimming.

THE SEA

From the high window I saw the sea!
It had a great heart
that throbbed with yachts & fish catches
& it had a strange color.

There was a tower once that was made of the sea,
I swear it,
a turning standing tower of water,
and a man lived inside,
wide-eyed, terrified & gleeful.
He is called
the man in the tower of the sea.

And he never comes out.
And he never went in, that he knows;
and the sounds of distant children
are his favorite flowers.

BIRD ON A SNOW-RIDGE

The storm blown out. Drifts
of three feet. Primp, primp, the bird
comes, eternally optimist for seeds!
And hand throws him
a scattering of sun-flowers. Primp, primp,
along the ridge, delicate messenger.
What do you put in your mouth, birdlet?
I have found, I have found
sunflower, sunflower seeds. Even today,
even in three feet of snow.
Even today I have found them.

EVENING

The phonographs turn in the mist
but the mist covers the world.

AIR FRANCE

In the avenues of Versailles
Morley looked for his distant love
in the shape of a jar, of an urn,
in a vase of brass or of stone.
In formal gardens
Morley fell apart & partially slept.
Wind-prodded, woke. & wept.

HERE

Here where the bird & the squirrel feed
together, in new snow.
Conspiratorial, three squirrels feed. *Four*.
Dusts of snow stipped from the branch
by birds who leap to feed
with intimate alterations of flight.
None fights in the shared air.
A dozen dark roads.

BROOKLYN

In the night a one-year-old child
calls for a taxi;
it is to take him to his mother

whose nipple browses above him.
He will swing
from those ropes of milk
like a small inhuman bell.

POWER FAILURE

Down in the valley,
the valley so low,
in black veils the officials
flicker with fear;
they dance up & down on the dumb wires
in glittery rage,
they blow bad music starwards,
they lift their harsh fingers into the black sky.

WITHOUT CONTRARIES IS NO PROGRESSION

'The blind children will sing tonight
at 7.15 in the hotel lobby.'

Birds
keep company on branches
with beads of rain.
They swing down for bread,
the rain drops.
O leave out meat for the silver fox,
O dig, my citizens, the fox out of your shoulder,
& name him, recognise him!

OZARK TO CEDAR RAPIDS

Flying now, under complete cloud cover, coming near.
Down there was where he hurried
to his love, North. Wisconsin there. Home
of the one white deer who fed once from his hand.
And he grazed with her in a white field.

Morley went to look for his horse
at the North Pole.
Nothing. And yet
one luminous nostril flashed in the air,
it was that of he!
The horse has been here & is gone
into thin air thinks our hero.
Better to smoke all kinds of hope
than horseless to be here.
O Morley, searching for thy horse
in air. In *air*. Poor fool, in air.

In an unlikely mood
Morley was blown by the wind
into his house
& found an eagle there.
'I was not expecting you' snarled the eagle,
getting up from the fireplace.
A lovely & naked woman with fair hair
was lying stretched out on the sofa,
having just come.
'You are back too soon' said the eagle
& flew up with a black anger
through the closed window, breaking
no glass.

The woman on the sofa wept,
turning to sand.

❊

Michael Morley met a beautiful & hungry woman
in a desert place.
He said to her: 'Your face is like a submerged cathedral, so
    beautiful.'
She said to him: 'I have not drunk good water for three
    months.'
They pranced on the sand for some time.
'You are hanging out in the wrong place' said Morley,
'This is no place for your hands to be a basilica.'
'That is correct' she said 'but I have a job here
waiting tables for Death. I cannot leave.'

A black vulture sat in a tree nearby
with red unpleasant eyes & a beak like a kitchen implement.
Morley felt helpless, like an aircraft.
'If only a string quartet' he murmured.
Instead he crunched a small village in his hands.
'Are you on the telephone?' he asked.
'Frequently' she replied. 'Call me with small bleeps.'
'If you were a slope
I would send my flocks to graze on you' said Morley.
'Thankyou' said the slope.
And then they parted.
But it would not be for long.

Pt. 2

Some smoke came out of Morley's reputation.
'O my reputation!' (Morley)
'Perhaps it is a signal for someone distant.' (she)
'If God sees it from His hills, He may think it is
a message for Him to come soon.

And I am in no hurry.' (Morley, fervently)
He unloosed her hair with a grave excitement.

The next time she met Morley
he was dressed as an admiral to go feed the ducks
in Central Park.
She matched him, stride for stride, down 79th St.
Some workmen saw Morley & fell into their hole.
As Morley & the lady walked
a Rolls-Royce filled with bread-crumbs
followed close behind them.
There was the vulture, *a lousy chauffeur.*

THE ATKINSON MORLEY HOSPITAL

Michael Morley's father died
in the Atkinson Morley hospital.

As father died
the men of the family stood in a circle,
Morleys all, surgeons all,
all of them famous surgeons.
Only *their* skills . . .

"I am a cedar of Spain" says one,
"pray die in my shade."
"I am Dr Pine" says another,
"and may not bend down."
And one: "I am Weeping Willow,
and would, if I could,
perform."
          But O Willow, poor Willow,
your fingers are weak & green,
your own bones weep.
Though you howl like a dog, like Lear,
you cannot save him.

And then did all Morleys weep,
useless the surgeons, thumb-strung, useless,
their tears like enormous robins.
Too late, late.

Nurse Birch,
shed down your leaves. Prince Blackberry,
Gorse,
O, say, Sir Thornbush,
won't you save,
can't you save
Morley my father?
Too soon he takes off his blood, sirs.
Sheik Shrub, Your Potency Rosetree,
help young old Morley now,
see, sirs, how he undresses in
his hall of mirrors on Calvary.

But stand, stand, stand,
all surgeons stand,
in blossom, unbandaged, their branches
clean, so helpless them all
& piteous to be seen.
                              And my mother jumps
up & down, up & down
on the roof of the family house.
"You can do anything you want!" she screams.
"You can do anything you want!"

And we come back to the house, & we will,
in the form of flames, or of darkness,
forever seeking our shapes, forever uneasy.

MORLEY & CAROLE McGUIRK

I was completing my third symphony when the rains began.
My neighbor, seizing the opportunity, washing his wife.
So many things going haywire.
I wanted to go to another planet like the rest of us.
But the little jewelled fox creeps over the scarlet frozen lake
with paws like hairy spatulas; a book of matches
is not the perfect honeymoon, certainly!
And then I remembered the last time I had leapt
over a convent wall! Always a sure sign of spring,
the frost taking out insurance,
the church bells with a new hat!
And so I am sending you my straw hat, Carole.

MORLEY & THE BLUE NUN

Cripes, Rhiney,
You've got some vineyards here!
Speechless barge of roast beef.
You'd better run about a bit, foreigner.
But the sun begins to set on my armor.

EUROPE

He runs because he is expected to run
he runs round Europe like a hot ticket

He runs into old squares & out of them
he runs because the little dry man is after him

He runs because the radar in the canyon says Run Run

He runs because this is comelier than dying

He runs because the cathedral's shadow grows big on his back
He runs because Europe struggles like a dark butterfly in his
    hand

Runs, he-who-runs-over-the-ice

Runs around old girls married now but not in, igloos
runs up here, here down, cinema, why, *meat pie*

Runs absolutely
runs because like waking up in a telephone

I have forgotten my lines, Sir

Runs because 'ha ha' and 'Yet Again'
runs because there is an error

Because the wind is bending all the people
because your friends are in the heavy zones

Because there is an error

He is past his best the harpsichord said, what, what?
because we go past Gotland, Åland & Bornholm

Runs because the sky shook her knees at me bloody
runs because rattle

Runs because we got past

Runs because the Danish wall & skaters turning into the Finnish
square & the astronaut is turning the child over in his hand
    who is
half of the world, *Yuri Gagarin who died*

Runs because of the last thing the hanged man does, *comes*

Runs by, north village, white tribe by the water

My hands like scissors on the past

NORTH WITH BARTOK

And could hear, far over
the dark water, Europe shaking
her scabbards, and on the tops
of crumbling cliffs the soft
hootings of English girls, calling
their men to arms.

IN THE FAMILY

A flower ran off the road
& vanished. A woman ran into the road,
deeply, up
to her neck. I followed her
with efforts. She had been
an aunt of mine. She had known
my father, & so on. She had known Africa.

I want you to tell me. My father is having
his birthday today on a planet;
why, his clothes are terrible!

Then the woman
begins. All jungles deepen. It is
quite a season. The man's back
steams, his eyes steam.
Then the woman has arrived.
The best parts of her body get off a bus!
What is the man to do? He wets
his whistle, & *runs*. No. He stands
there, still, stick-
like, dry, constant, pastor-
al.

Sun over the hill. Daughters
under the bridge. This is love,
bring it, & shiver.
This is what the world is.

POWER FAILURE

Morley's lights went out.
All of a sudden, with a plunk of silence.
And so Morley discovered the moon.
Yellow & enormous, it was glowing
just over the black ridge; Morley
had not noticed it.

The whole valley below him
went dark. And he saw the shaky
light of candles in his nearest
neighbors' house, through the trees.
Not only Morley's lights then,
but the lights of all.

How good to rediscover the moon
thought Morley, blacked out on his ridge.
How quiet the flames sway! While the
meat cooks. 'I shall have to baste the meat by flashlight'
his guest's wife said. 'Yes' thought Morley.

Out in the snow, did the fox stop
when the human houses went dark? Like the lungs
of a man who hear the great heart
cease, and wonder, waiting for orders.
Is the whole body closing down?

Morley's lights went out. & the valley's
with him. And many men's, who sat
in the dark like he. Friends of the dark,
thought Morley, be in your houses & wait.

The cat wants to go into the fireplace.
The friends wish to gather, but the dark forestalls them,
such dark, thinks Morley, in its own failure.
And ah the power fails,
ah the failure of it.
The guest's wife shines
the flashlight, while the guest & friend
makes the fire.
It is Roy doing it, & Margaret shining.

Feverishly the officials are working
to find the failure. In my veins,
thinks Morley, in my veins. Orchards
darken; each in his own
landscape leaks. And a great moon rises
in the brain, in the mind of man & of Morley,
& its yellowness tells him
it is here to stay.
We must be brave in our dark.

CALM, CALM

Calm, calm, a great calm came.
Morley wanted it.
Everyone else wanted it, for him & for themselves.
And so a great calm came.

Each man has washed his house!
They have got up early
like sailors scarlet at dawn,
& they have with mops & strange warm cloths
done their good business;
see now how the wet wood shines!

O fine green house where Morley lives,
white fur of wolf & Snow Queen,
& true forest with its wind-kings of emptiness.
In such calm
drapes are drawn across great windows without sound;
and through air flies
even the broken bird,
he with the least wing. Each creature
walks shining on the ice of his life
in the darkest wood even. The furnace

gathers to a pure roar in the night;
& pain flees from all portraits; even the pained
dead man on the wall is bland; the heart
has the thump of a friend in the dark.
And all in a great calm lie.

MORLEY AS PILOT

Merry Christmas. This is the captain speaking.
I am very drunk. So, we are all up a tree!
There's a cloud! The stars fell through

the long dark shopping bag of night.
I am waiting for a camel to turn up,
I am waiting for the wind to go past.
Our speed is favorable everybody!
We will not get stuck in the snow at this speed!
With all my clothes off it is much easier to fly.
A dog just went past on a chocolate!
My life seems little enough.
Well you are all soft enough.
I hope you are all wide open.
I hope you are all my piano.
Did you enjoy your dinner? I heard
its screams, I was in England then, near an archway.
The lightning whispered me her telephone number,
the thunder promised me a massage
back at the black hotel.
This plane is a black hotel!
I am a fox with my tail in my brain!
The wheels are full of water.
The wings are to be sent back because we have done with them.
Everybody! Let us pray! I am completely flooded!
I am kneeling in the rice-field of the cabin!
I am the baker in winds!
Engines, I will buy you the socks of communism!
I have to go now. *This plane will from now on
be flown entirely by apples.*

New Milford, Connecticut/Ocean Avenue, Brooklyn
December 1968—May 1969

RUST FROM THE MARVELOUS ENGINES

FOR LYNNE CASTONGUAY

"My name is Herman Melville, I write fish stories."
                    (Kenneth Koch, in conversation)

1

In the gospel according to Saint Leaf I read
there was snow on your belt.
Or how, when you crossed the Atlantic like an opera,
your breasts, like sopranos, the horror of commodores,
bruised no shipping. You know how I love to be
a lithe idiot in the rigging.

When I saw that the swimmers were browning in the rock-pool
out of the sheer excellence of the atmosphere,
I marched into the Swedish field for consolation
only to be made hay of by a picnic of violins;
you bailed me out.

When I was accosted by the cop who wanted
the TV dinner so badly he was prepared to kill for it,
a small bird peed on him from high up
and the sunset turned into the only muscles he had.
Thankyou for the bird, I recognised your markings.

You know how you come and go between the trees,
you know how I love that.

Lynne, you know how the snow
swells through the formal idea. We drove past
ANGIE'S TAKE-OUT CLAMS on the way to Boston's
        ghoulish airport.
I did not want to let you go. O I held
the airport to my lips, and sipped it;
it was crummy, of course, like all oysters.
I did not want to let you go.

When the champagne came up out of the floor
you did not even panic.
'Be grateful' you said. And
'We are not even religious.'
Did we drink together. Or,
did we not.

If you smiled from Asia I would hear you.

When Alexander was playing with jewelry in the dark
I hid in a chalk quarry with a distant cousin
while the casualties from the heaviest Japanese snowstorm
gathered in the bookstore at midnight to share arrows generally
and work out the scent of a dwarf on paper.

When the king of ideas advanced through the wood
you fed him an image and he went away.
When I found myself admiring the thunder-tampered hill
you raised no objections.
When I told you you had been seen with the small princes
        of milk
you moved to Brooklyn Heights, you handed me
Babylon in my sandwich.
When I was so unhappy in the State Forest
you arranged to raze it.

These are the least of them.

2

From rivalling ditches, the friends extend their hands.
The sun's peculiar harness swells in the air. Lynne,
at this time of evening, with everything
gold, red, the deep blue of horizons, I can see
the can-openers beginning their ascent of the mountain;
let us all wish them luck.

Three quotations:
1/ "I have found an onion in Moscow that is probably
my brain."
2/ "It will be so nice to return to Lapland and perhaps
at weekends
we can resume the search for my ear."
3/ "I have never heard a plane coming in so low as my
grandfather's marriage."

One evening, the moon
struggled in the far pasture; guilt
spread all over the field.
The wasp of hope spat at me,
the bird broke from her thicket with a sneer,
scarlet, scarlet all over, flooding the air!

We have done fast turns in the dark
as the farm wandered out of us singing;
O we have eaten our food on the fences of ridicule,
we have arrived with our brains combed back,
we have turned, damaged in air, plucky as experts,
rising, always rising.

I have told you, the tree grows
in the abandoned car; the quartet
are terribly ill but are playing still. The waiter
walks into the ground carrying his wound.
I have heard
the little children in oilskins
and seen
the glitter of winter light on peculiar rivers;
in the vaster tundra of the sky
I have heard the wind making its winter journeys.

In their webs of coal
the spider miners wither. In the night,
the eye of the dog is washed fresh;
in the night, the dog turns away.

In the yellow glade the old man
threw the boy away, in Switzerland.
And I have seen, to my own satisfaction,
actual flames on the mountain.

3

Here they come, the brain-captains,
the spoilers, the swamps by proxy.

I touched the woman, she was
gas, she came apart in my hands. The woman
climbed a rope to escape me, but the rope
was an odor. We ate
a meal together, we offered
bread to the waiter, dipped in batter. The bread
was called Little-gun-of-no-escape.
The waiter took out one eye, it was labelled 'Plum'.
I have told you, the ugly man
runs in his own moonlight.

I have seen you asleep
in a strong wind;
you swung like a lamp in a rectory,
you lay out under the stars like a coachman, untouchable.
I saw you, small and silver, on the limbs
of a great tree; were you dancing there?

I hand you a card,
I hand you an eye on a tray;
I have seen an airplane weep
its passengers from the sky,
I have seen the eye of a city
close its lash of brick with an immense sigh,
I have poised on a roof-garden with a friend from Kansas
and seen a horse balancing over s swamp,
with a bucket of apples,
of wires & ointment, of the arms of babies.

On the mattress the water floats,
five people swim there.
The Japanese manufacturer of new islands,
the brother-in-law of casualties,
the Israeli gunner,
the man in the suit of shell-fish,
the combination Mexican with the slum on his lip.

Well, I saw the firemen coming
out of your apartment. I saw the king
making off down the street, history
running out of him like sand,
I saw the great building come down, I saw
the butcher with his manacles and wrists
and the dancers who were passing plants
to each other in their sleep, President
Jekyll, President Hyde, shadowy twins
vaulting the dark Atlantic.

She has a way to walk across a room.
She has a way to turn from you in sleep,
like a forest being cleared,
like the annexing of Malaysia,
like a closet found full of dead fish who missed their birthdays.

The person lubricates the poem.
You thank the farmer, who has, after all,
damp hands. The woman
flows across the room;
frigates, lunar modules, the Baltic duties.
The woman knocks
on the door of the bathroom, are you shaving
with your fingers, or why
are your hands at your throat?

When the cedar fell over I mopped it up,
with a blue sponge,
with a green sponge,
with a pink sponge,
with a yellow sponge.
Love is a stain on the air.

In the exhilaration of the deep idea
I saw her changing her dresses endlessly,
in the company of sunlight, among trees
and construction workers,
bringing goats to the hungry revolutionaries,
soaping the third airplane,
loaning herself to the pilots of hopeless causes.

She is unto herself.
She says 'I will come back to you.
I will be there.' And slips
into the hollow tree, and zips it up,
snail for all seasons.

Insanity, I have heard your cousins on the battlements;
Fear-of-myself, I have written your name in the sand.

4

Lynne, what to do with the dark ships?
Let us include the agonies peculiar to the genre.
Well no. I will drive you to work now.
No breakfast; the stomach
ticks like a clock.
The veils come off, the veils remain and kill.
How far is it to Brooklyn? Not far.
It is not far to Connecticut, not really,
it is not far to Roy and Margaret's,
it is not far to Whitewater or Wild Rice, North Dakota;

the chicken weeps in the telephone booth,
the black snow drifts;
the forms of the snow are restless,
the forms of the farm are heated;
the English plead for their wounds back, the French glitter;
the bull murmurs from his swanky nest,
menace is revving her marvelous engines
near the Canadian border.
It is not far to ostrich,
not far to the roads of ridiculous pleasures.
An orange. Half a duck on a plate. Aerials.
I have decided. I will wait for you to come back.

New York City
12/4/68

CHERRY

The bird has pecked with its beak
at the forehead of the man, marking

him with its scar.
For the man is all cherry now.

One comes in with a ticket
purchased (o hands

at the window),
one with the wind on his back.

What the pencils write,
when the buses leave,

who owns this whole estate,
green valley, enormous moon,

who leaves food on the sofa,
why the dark flag lowers

among dandelions. Cherry hangs
from a window, it is lunch-time,

who owns the earth,
girls under the trees,

who walks your own path,
green valley, enormous moon,

will you have a saviour,
the snake that flies,

leaves, the engines burning,
lamps revolving on stands,

have given up lighting,
the lamps,

'nobody owns us'
the wind says, turning

the leaves,
'there is no one here'

the orchestra rehearses in the shed,
the bridal dust of engines,

there are
the scars in the blouse, the tractor,

there is the earth
if you want it, ploughing,

but first the damage, the ownership,
you just settle the ownership,

the damage. And the ship
drifts on, that summer lake,

like a lamp gone out; own
up to it, cherry, burnt

fruit, the beak, the bird
on the sofa, the snake

that flies.
Green valley. Enormous moon.

ELEGY

For Kate Houskeeper and Elie Siegel, two students of Bennington College, who died in an automobile accident, April 7, 1969

Birds on the branch outside my window.
I wish they were Elie,
I wish they were Kate.

I wish they were taking a shower
or going to lunch. I wish Elie was
making more music, notes of her own,
lovely, serious and slim, expertly
on the violin. I wish Kate was
arranging her curls. Kate, I will miss
your curls, where you sat, in the front
of the class, listening.
But the girls have gone into the dark.

I wish you were vain,
I wish you had time to touch yourselves,
in front of mirrors,
in front of lovers.
I want Elie just once more
to lay her hands on Mozart,
to play as I saw her play,
intent, at just one concert.
I do not want you thrown
out of a car, your lives,
an evening in April, when I was driving
the same way, back, back here.
But I arrived. And am alive.
I stopped once to watch
the last of light over the hills.
Maybe you went by me then;
for sure you went by me for ever.

The day of your death I fell asleep
in the afternoon; and woke, afraid,
dreaming I had run down
the dark ladders of afternoon,
down, always down; and was glad to find
no wife lay at my side, to share
in my fear.

But you further
and faster than I, life saying
these I do not want, these
I do not choose to have, to learn, to make
more music, to love, I do not want
these hands poring over my face,
I will cast them forever.

And today, the Spring lake
bright like blue ploughland, a warmer
wind through the trees,
the evergreens rocking and dipping their limbs
and even the rocks putting out little hands inside,
here are we who must make
music for you now,
from the cello, the shining violin,
lament for the makers, for the makers are gone,
but the music goes on.

But for you,
all making, all music, all love,
lying down for ever
with the earth that is newer by far
than ever before.

And birds on the branch beside my window,
singing too soon, singing too late;
in April, birds with their strange new song.
I wish they were Elie. I wish they were Kate.

4/8/69
Bennington

LETTER TO NICK & KATE

Dear Nick & Kate, I have found
great sanity again in gardening,
unbelievable, gathering in leaves,
burning newspapers, sweeping
the porch of my own house,
far from the many overhead.
I am bright gardener again,
the children know me & my new car,
dog of dry puddles, happy
in the litter of autumn in April.

The glasses of afternoon
fill with the gold light.
Spiders ride, the clean children play,
no dead girls drift in the mind,
there is no damage.

COAL

Boys throwing lumps of coal into the dark.
Lumps sailing through the dark.
This road many of us walked home from school.
The click of insects loving in the rhododendrons.
Schoolgirls taking off their blouses inside bushes.
Lumps of coal sailing through the dark.
Bullies holding a face in two inches of puddle.
How the girls make the boys come in the bush.
Boys who have not loved throwing coal out into the dark.
The wind wiping clean. Hold us, hold us, for we are
Lumps of coal sailing through the dark!

STORM THOUGHTS & CHILDREN

The children consulted thin clocks.
All the light was mopped up by the strange
town-owners.
No one thought it queer the storm came.
When a plane crashed for lack of food
the school children buried the accident.
In a one-room building they led away
their lives.
As men wipe their towns away.
Lots of the children looked out of the windows
a great deal of the time.
Their thoughts went slowly
out of print. Gradually
the glass in the windows fell asleep.

VERMONT, JUNE

I think I am only being kept
alive by my hunger.

A thick white light falls
in these side-roads. Where a barn

is collapsed in a vicious
wind, I give off shadows. Where

cattle flicker by their river
I am gathered aside into

the thick pasture of no answer.
Hopefully, I am cut in half,

hopefully led astray. There is
an amputation in the air.

HIGH LEVEL

I looked through her violin, it was
the microscope she played at her shoulder; through it

I saw a map of the floor of the Indian Ocean
where music crawled in fixed ranges,

pods of rock, stems of the continents; all
the world was her instrument, & through it I saw

the blackness outside, all the blackness
her instrument, the tower, the

microscope. It froze at her shoulder.
Or, if you want, it was burning.

THE PEACH TERRACE

For George & Amy

The bishop has narrowly escaped
the hands of George's trees again.
How his mitre glitters with paranoia!

To sit beneath this tree
is an act of God, like a blue peach

kneeling, to pray in this sunlight,
a log in her harness of wine.
My neighbors are knitting small wools of rumors
all around me. To sit

on this terrace is to be a shepherd,
bruising no one. From here, my blessing
to the world & urban areas, from here

my sticky little thoughts take off, each
like a hairbrush with a mission to comb

the storms of God. On this terrace
I write my decree for George. If only he

would swoop to the rail for a minute, relinquishing
Amy, I could throw
the crumbs of appointment at him from deep
in the valley of the white & invaluable white glove.

TOWARD A POEM
ON THE DEATH OF BISHOP PIKE

"And I think a man should find his Holy Land where he
first crawled on the floor . ." (W. B. Yeats)

Happy here

A bush

& near

The gate opens, someone walks into the garden

The moon in a kneeling position

Boys playing near the edge of the water,
throwing a little dried ball of soap between them
Throwing & catching, pieces of it breaking off

The sea kneeling down between countries

I believed my own sweat to be an important geography
and I fell down to worship it.
I looked up and saw
the kings fall over the cliff, one by one,
out of the mothers.
I saw the geese falling too,
a lovely dropping machinery of geese,
like a waterfall for Wordsworth.
I am what one man is who is too hot.

I have got the letters of my name wrong.
The k goes soft, then it's an f.
If I tie my laces up, I'm an African.
I hear a plane but I wanted it to be a boiled egg.
O peoples, mothers, O war-makers,
my left hand is a little place,
my right hand won't drown anybody.
If I am where I think I am

I am near the Dead Sea,
I am ten miles from Bethlehem.

❋

Nobody knows me,
ha ha. This is my place,

I'll name it. Place I fell down in,
from, into, on, place

of sun's muck, & rock.

❋

A bishop tries to climb

❋

The dead have their ambulances too.
Also their supermarkets, and their scholarships.
Do you want to see their sculptures?
At night, at night, in the spaces
between stars, made of the rain.

The old battleship covered with cobwebs.
The aircraft carrier covered with playing fields,
and boys running and playing there.

You would have thought the good doctor . . .
But choosing to go on. He had left

clues on his trail, articles
of clothing, spectacles, a small case.

And we must send the old battleship
back into her webs,

and we must move back into the heart of things.

❋

There was a nest on a branch
and I saw a bird rise up out of it,
horribly, because its wings were made of iron,

its whole body was too heavy,
and schoolboys were holding on
to its beak; part of their game
was the difficult rise of this bird.

I am not vain now.
I have whatever crowns.
They can crawl for me for I care.
The sound of the Dead Sea is like nothing else.
I like, I am where I ought to be.
There is an army looking for me.

When my wife came to my side
I was in the pool of a garden.
I said: My love, I do not want
the evening to come. My wife said;
you have not said anything.
You have not said anything at all.

Here's an astonishing butterfly.
His wings are like stained glass, red and black.
His black head is smothered with white spots.
On my back like this.
I can see the universe like this.
In the wood, two trees down.
One I run under, one that stops me.
Smelly doll.
Iron tears leave my face,
my face lightens.

Happy here

The heavily bandaged helicopter
is lowered into the well.
Black water, black water.

Are you disturbed? Are you disturbed?
What kind of machine is your grass?

It is a child
in her Gethsemane of dolls;
this is my father, the River Jordan,
and she is my mother, the thorn.

Why have you held the huge toy
in front of the child?

Welcome to a new kind of classroom.

Here is the palm of your hand.
Why do you drop on all fours?
Here's a map of your eyes,
here's the hot terrain.
You're on Mars.
Little minerals go by on legs.

The heat sent her priests, they're saying
mass on each grain of dust.
Goodbye the army of flàvor.

The fly cruises through the air,
he's a destroyer.
His black machinery afloat on the heat.
He flies with the sandals of disease.

I am following in Jesus' footsteps

I have no regrets

I am too hot

WALES

I am gathering wood with my brother in the dusk.
It is New Year's Eve, we are in Wales.

Both saw the fire on the hill. Someone's house is burning.
Or, it is the garbage. It is snowing. The snow falls on the
snow. The snow is falling on the sea. Hisses.

We are by the sea. An old mansion has fallen down & is filled
with wind. When my brother blesses me I am an orchard near
the sea. My trees are very black & flattened. The sea wind has
bent my head. But my brother stands like an abbey of young
wood.

But now for the fire we milk the forest. We pour the amputa-
tions down into the valley. We walk back toward the cottage
with wood on our shoulders. We follow the funeral path of the
old valley.

In the night our fire of young wood burns. It lights up the last
faces of the year. Certainly, there are ghosts hurrying over the
bridge.

Later, there is the future, like an axe seen at the window.

THE DAUGHTERS OF MUSIC

"And the daughters of music shall be brought low"

The daughters of music took their hearts from the loft
They put eyelashes on their hearts & ate them
The daughters of music rolled their hearts down a hill

Who are these men coming up? They are the beaters & searchers
Their children are with them, they have brought baskets
They set out before it was even light, with sandwiches
These are the men who are looking for something that's lost
They walk in line

The daughters of music paint on the doors of the snow
They are tying ribbons round the rain as it falls
They give birth on the teeter-totter & the park swing

The men are walking over the earth with wands
Something in the ground tugs at their little wands & encourages
    them

The daughters of music are walking out of the sea now
The lobsters sweeten in their hands
The daughters of music lift up their claws to the sun

The men are sitting in fields, they are eating their puddings
They are resting, they are exhausted, they are run down
Their fingers graze in the harsh advice

The daughters of music can be heard through the thin walls
They are crying out, they are caught in the branches, they need
    changing
The daughters of music are clinging to the rockets as they rise

Under the hill beyond wands the hearts are in flood
They are a crop, they gush & lift up their legs
The earth is unwound from them & they flow

The daughters of music dream of the buried
The men have gone, they are coming down the paths
The camera sweetens their search, they are left with images

The daughters of music part the earth with their hands,
they are looking
Under the earth the hearts are kissing, they will kiss each other
for ever
The daughters of music are sharpening twigs with their crowns
Under the sea the hooks are kissing
See, see, how the daughters of music breathe on the water

THE DEAD BEAR

O bear

In your mortuary of wind!

You hang & swing
from your teeth from the cord
from the pole from the tree

O never hang me like this black
bear in Minnesota, will you

Hung, four days & nights,
hardened

Two logs jammed there
keep your belly open to dry

2

In the forest the wolves run
their fluent packs,
I cannot handle them

But you
as the snow falls
I can come to you

O bear
as the ice clamps the lake now
& moon walks on the whiteness
I can come to you
where you hang
between two trees

& as other living
stand & sniff
stand in harmony like horses

I can reach to you
Rap, rap
like a door you've hardened
Rap, rap
I can bang on you
as I could not
when you moved & lived
I can touch you

only in death

as only in death
I can touch so many more

CAVE PAINTINGS

For Robert & Judith Sward

I saw the children scratch
our pictures on the wind.
They come & go,
the eternally strange children.
Jail us, please.

I saw the children throw
the water away, our faces on it
like moons. I saw them
draw us, carve
on the flesh of a tree,
the skin of a new car.
The fathers breathe in those stones.

Do they master us now,
is it magic?
Those are animals they draw.
But it is our fire in their hands,
they etch us ourselves.
They throw us away then,
and our breath in the stones.
The faces skip on the water.

2

There are frogs in the pond,
there are peepers,
but the children are there too,
with their voices,
and the dead unborn child is there,
his scratches, *his* vocabulary
in the stones of exterior brothers,
who marks us his image
of what his world might have been,

in the flesh of the living
tree, the skin of machine.
The dead child breathes in those stones.

O wasp, do you wait
in the sea-wind? Toy in the barn,
are you ready? Little
miner, small sheriff
in his parish of scars. And the signals
in the stones stop. Silence
in the museum. And *she* knocks
on the door of the empty villa
by the sea. The children play
elsewhere. The pulse
lies dead in the stones.

3

Then who will walk
with the dead child
in the pasture of many stars?
But no no says the birds,
not even the birds, bells
on the branch that wither, as he
in his village of water
will not ring
ever. Scratch, scratch,
& your brothers & sisters, their
hungry stones, draw
you, us, those
moons among the living. On their surfaces
they are putting us down.
Trapped. Traveler. O target.

SIONED MARY WATKINS, WELCOME

Tiny skull in the snow
O turtle
Small snow-lady, shell

Even the wolf's warm

No feathers No
smoke

Little knife
hung from the moon

Morley wants
to say hallo, too

Hallo, bird

You have given me something to feed

12/17/69

EUROPE

For Alex and Hanna, Christian and Ulrich

1

What a scattering of shadows on the snow
on the path to the door!

You are caught
in the branches of Europe again. Around,
white nests of Denmark.

A new light comes out of the mouths of friends.
They make fresh meals. There are new lamps.
What strange speech they have.

In this house is a friendly & tangible ghost.
What vaguer shapes
cross the Atlantic & wander abroad,
haunting America.

To have the snow of Europe
melt in your hand again, after so long.

Tock, tock,
gold axe of the clock.

A bird dives up to a branch,
dives down again.
Who shall we be today?

2

You stand in Europe again melting back into it
There is wind in the farm by the sea
Marriages go by like buckets
Small concerts of neighbors' noises
What do we wash the dishes with *with your bright eyes*

You have the papers to be in Europe again
You are in the vicinity of many places & ghosts
The toys are crowded
The mouths of the children are filled with small teeth
Look at the statue, *birds sit on the gentleman*

There goes a line of birds over the sky
Someone looks out of a skylight at you
Tick the snow says tock the clock
And so a statue goes by on a bicycle, slowly
The axe falls forever through the air.

3

In the closet the candlestick is burning.
Darkness falls in rings from your clothing.

And you can forget the poems
that have run away from you in horror
like headless birds in the dark
you have not quite killed,

because in this house & place
there are good fresh ghosts,
there are small & near ones here.

Fingers on the guitar,
on the Andreas Christensen piano.
The unborn children walk on the music.
In white nightgowns,
the children are here to complete the poems.

Birkerød
January 1970